THE SILENT ROAD

MUSKAN BALI

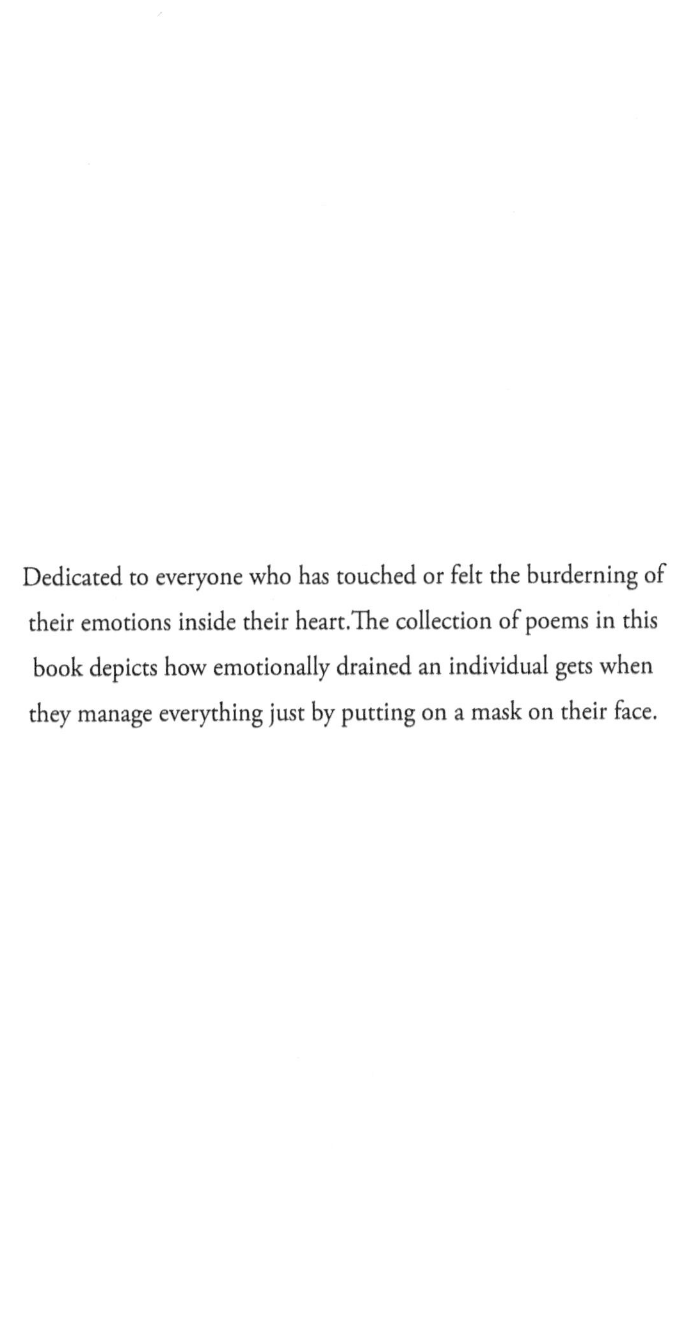

Dedicated to everyone who has touched or felt the burderning of their emotions inside their heart. The collection of poems in this book depicts how emotionally drained an individual gets when they manage everything just by putting on a mask on their face.

Contents

Contents

Acknowledgements

A leader alone cannot complete the goal unless he/she gets a strong support system.I do not believe I have done enough in my life and I aim to grow more but whatever I have done,it could not have been possible without the people around me. I would want to start by thanking the person who made me who I am or maybe wants me to be an even better person. My mother Mrs.Hemlata Bali for her constant support and help during this writing process.Thankyou so much guiding me always.Without your constant support I am nothing.

I would also like to thank my father Mr.Yogesh Kumar Bali and my sister Ms. Mehak Bali for always motivating me to do something different.

A special token of thanks to my friends Aakriti Lodha and Swati for helping throughout the process.

My friends are my critics.I would like to thank Aaryan Dabra, Pratichi, Aastha, Shivani, Jaya, Sanchita, Pritvi, Jagriti, Meghna, Kirupa and everyone else who helped me in anyway possible.

Lastly, I would like to thank God for giving me enough and giving me the power to write all my poems.

Prologue

Maybe in the parallel universe it was us and not me

Letter For The Readers

Dear Reader,

We are all burdened with our emotions and as we all grow we learn the magical art to hide them under a beautiful smile.And this is the saddest part of our lives.

The poems in this book are written from a second person's perspective.The perspective which all of us have sometime or other felt and it is beautiful.

It is absolutely normal for us to hide our emotions but it is just us who know how to manage such circumstances.

May this book open up a not-so challenging perspective to you.

Thankyou so much for taking out your precious time to read by work and I hope this book open up your happy perspective towards life.

Happy Reading !
Muskan Bali

1. For once

The wind which touched you touches me for once,
for once your fragrance gets absorbed in my body,
for once you untangle my hair,
for once you show me your true colours,
for once you cry as I collect your droplets in my hand,
for once you smile just to help my heart beat a bit fast,
for once you come foreward,
for once you hug me hard,
as I touch you I see God infront of my eyes,
If you live- I live,
If you die- I die,
for once, for once, just for once.

2. The mask

I wore a mask infront of people,
So that whatever is in my heart doesn't come out as I talk,
I went on a journey with my friends to find true happiness,
forgetting my true happiness was left behind in the journey of
life.
Staying with everyone- wearing a fake facemask I earned
everyone,
But when I went by in my room at night removed that mask,
I cried my heart out,
and I asked myself
Is this life?
wearing a fake smile infront of others
Is this life?
Trying to learn to live
Is this life?
keeping all your sufferings inside your heart
Is this life?

3. Broken dreams

I used to feel happy whenever I saw you,
my heart used to get a reason to beat faster just by senseing you
around,
I used to get a huge smile on my face whenever I used to think
about you,
I always had a desire to get dressed up only for you,
I started believing again in fairytales,
I was happy in the dreamworld I made all by myself,
every dream has an end,
but my heart is still not groomly ment,
I collected all my broken dreams in a cloth and went ahead in
the journey of life,
with a hope that one day they might be fixed back and I could
start dreaming again.

4. Hidden emotions

Some things are still embedded inside my heart,
some things are still hidden in my mind,
sometimes I just want to forget everything and say whatever I
have inside my heart,
what would you say after hearing this is something which scares
me hard,
my silence easily potrays what I feel inside my heart,
my heart stops beating whenever I see you with someone else,
what magic have you done on me?
In my prayers I often see your face besides mine.

5. Talking to myself

Whenever I am alone at night I often think about you,
I could not be with you is something which triggers me too,
I always wanted to meet you,
but what will I say once I see you scares me too,
I wish I could have this superpower,
that I could just change whatever has happened,
I wish I could have been your friend rather than being your
lover,
this realisation triggers my heart and my mind,
staying away from you still triggers my heart and my mind,
whatever was in my heart came out,
the relationship which could have been of friendship could never
be.

6. Let it go

When people want things they can't have,
they forget to live and laugh,
they force their life in moid,
which leaves them alone and scared.
One cannot set his spirit free,
if one is locked into what his life must have been,
many things aren't left to chance,
because life is not as smooth as dance.
Shut out the sun's pure light,
because now the life is not so bright,
accepting hard the reality it gives,
the lesson's true for all the lives.
With light sometimes comes rain,
but our heart is still in pain,
but this is our part of life,
to know the range from joy to strife.

7. Heartfelt

Have you ever heard my bleeding heart, roaring your name?
Did you ever feel my glances touching your face?
When ever you pass by, the gush of the wind that traverses
between us,
is the light of my heart, to sustain in a world without you.
I never knew what true love is until I started loving you,
without any expectations or hope but some form of satisfaction.
Deeply rooted love for both of us, yet I singly possessed all of it,
no gifts, no love yet I celebrated my life each day,
I struggle to exist but let my warmth into a deep meaningful
love,
my eyes are welled up and tears drew canvases on the pillow
every night,
Oh dear ! thats the reality of my life.

8. The leftover

People say whatever happenes- happenes for good,

forget everything and move on in life- This is life,

but if it was so easy to let go of things, feelings and people in our

life,

would I even have my heart beating this fast?

I really dont have a lot to earn in my life honestly,

I really do not have a lot to loose in my life except of my self-

respect,

but even today when I feel lonely- I always ask myself,

Will my heart beat the same way it used to beat?

Will it put so much efforts for others as it did for you?

Will it trust others so easily as my heart did to you?

This thing shatters the heart,

keeping me away from you- you break my heart.

9. You

I feel a sense of discomfort within me,
and I do not even find a relevant reason as to why I sometimes
feel lost,
my heart gets a reason to beat faster seeing you around,
and at the same time it gets a reason to stop realising the fact
youre not around me,
I feel lost-I feel alone,
I feel like crying every single morning,
what magic have you done on me,
that even when I wish to work you come in my dreams to stop
me,
your beautiful black eyes,
your gloomy cute smile,
your magical charm,
all of it says loud to me- you're special,
You're special for me,
I hope one day I be blessed with this magical superpower,
that whatever I feel inside my heart,
I keep all of it to myself,
by not being your lover,
but atleast by being your friend.

10. The potrayal

I remember our journey right from start,
the tragic one with initial pleasure,
those feelings were like as if they were broken and extant,
I could not server from the vibrations the giggles you gave me
when you comforted me,
I cannot forget the snuggling out of the house,
the cafe diaries and the texts and the calls,
I omit to forget you- forget your touch and your warmth,
you coloured my soul,
the distances between us felt void,
the only drop of nourishment flows through you,
you are my God- you are my Almighty,
your little deportment cherished me into your love over and over
again.

11. Its Hard

Its hard for me,
Its hard for me to smile infront of you whenever I see you with
someone else,
Its so difficult for me to show nothing matters to me,
Its hard for me to hide my emotions,
Like a sea you came into my life,
an unplanned entry I must say,
but from the time you entered my life,
I learnt to smile and to slay,
I could feel every bit of my senses,
and could also get a motivation to get dressed,
you are my magic,
you are my charm,
I dont know what faith I have on destiny,
that today also I believe we can be one.

12. Ready to fall again

If falling was not as painful as it is,
I could have the courage to fall again just for you,
If this time you were there to catch me,
I could have fallen again,
If you said that you'll alone,
I would want to fall again,
If you promised me that you won't leave me again,
I would want to fall again,
If once you knew how much I wanted to fall,
I could have fallen again,
If you had let out that smile once,
I could have fallen again,
I am prone to falling,
Again I'll fall,
and wait till I get discovered,
falling is beautiful and,
I am ready to fall again.

13. Unheard

In the darkest of nights,
I easily see the splashes of your light,
the smoke of the cigar,
the smell of your flower,
and the closeness of dreaming night,
I was still addicted to your mind my honey,
In the middle of a dark night,
I felt you touch me on my head,
your soft touch left me clueless,
the same way a budding bird tries finding its way,
love never looked so beautiful to me,
but you made one,
your essence have my heart tanginess,
to remember throughout,
that our very own story had a darkest side,
and my deepest feeling for you,
was unheard like a virgin flower.

14. Beauty of life

I am in the dark,
I am away from all the lights,
I do not feel anything at sometimes,
I sometimes feel scared-I sometimes feel lost,
this probably is the story of my life,
I have people and I go out,
and I do try sometimes to find happiness in my way,
but this is the beauty of my life that whenever I try I fail,
I fail everytime to get myself start a new phase,
Our books are filled with a lot of chapters,
some good and some not,
but the chapter have you become of my life,
I am never able to change,
this is the beauty of my life.

15. The road

Everything around me was and cool,
nothing hot as sheep with wool,
I went alone along the lonely road,
with the big block like a troad,
all alone all alone !!
The same paradigm I followed each day,
but my life decided to take a new turn this day,
I met the person I liked,
and sooner and later that changed my life,
months and days passed by,
but I could not see the person stand by,
then my look took some way,
about which I have nothing to say,
few days it was what it could last,
but learning starts by understanding your own past,
I decided to take a decision,
to never make someone in my priority vision,
Meanwhile I will say in an overtone,
all alone all alone !!

16. The wait

I am ready to wait here,
for the beauty blue sky for me,
for your worst suspicions to die for me,
for you to try and make me cry.
I am ready to wait here,
for the ice to melt,
for the roses to be beautifully smelt,
for you to once feel what I felt.
I am ready to wait here,
for the moments to pass,
for the memories to last,
for you to break that one glass.
I am ready to wait here,
for the ships to sail through the sea,
for the clock to strike three,
for you to believe in me.
I am ready to wait here,
for your silence to break,
for your usual soul to shake,
for your love to wake.

17. Ignored

There was a time when I was adored by many,
now is the time when I am ignorned by many,
there was a time when I was respected by many,
now is the time I am hated by many,
there was a time when people wanted my company,
now is the time there is noone to accompany,
there was a time when I was the one,
now is the time when I am noone,
maybe I am not the one who deserves any company,
from reel to real I am witnessing this tragedy,
How do I stop this downfall turning into painful agony,
please come back all maybe I am waiting for you all patiently.

18. Darkness

There is some form of darkness in each and everyone of us,
which we happily consider as a fuss,
its thoughts makes us go nuts,
and the people around us are ready to consider it as a cuss,
How could you possibly enjoy the sun?
when in the darkness you haven't run,
darkness let that sink in,
let it prink you like a pin,
but should always remember to never give it up,
because the journey of thousand miles has just begun,
Journey? because it is inevitable,
remember you can never it like a label,
from a day or a night can you disable?
By ignorance for sometime it is possible,
but like in poles it makes your life very unstable,
accepting is the first step of solving it,
solving it sometimes makes us feel it,
In daylight anyone can spark,
even a mosquitoe can leave a mark,
but this spark is not visible in the dark,
to be the kind of this amusement park,
like a lion you have to hunt in the dark,

once you start to enjoy both these part,
you become somone who is inpossible to tear apart,
it is also an art,
practising it over and over again till you get a kick start.

19. Magical eyes

Are you a magician ?
Do you know the art to control people?
Oh God! Right from the time I see you,
I see something in you,
Something very different- something very beautiful,
and something extremely wonderful,
I can easily see flowers in your eyes,
I can easily see comfort in your smile,
are you like others,
or are you someone different,
this question still stays a mystry in my heart,
but their is something in you,
because of which I smile each day,
each day just thinking about you.

20. No smiles left

Noone knows- noone will ever come to know,
that I live with a bleeding heart,
my bleeding heart everday misses you,
it everyday just cries for you,
but it has become so strong,
that it has mastered the art of its feeling from you,
it smiles infront you,
it shows you how strong it is,
but deep down inside,
it is totally shattered,
it looses its control whenever it sees you with someone else,
I believe our story is like a rose,
as beautiful as it looks like,
as much hurtful it is to me.

21. In the way of life

Sometimes I lay thinking about you,
I wish I could turn back time,
back to the time when we used to share smiles together,
I know it was always supposed to be the way it has become now,
I certainly didn't have a lot of expectations also tho,
but however a part of me always did,
I am ready to wait for you to come back,
with your very warm and beautiful smile,
the ones I wrote poems about,
the ones you never liked,
I always knew you'd kill for your dreams,
and I never saw myself as a part of them,
a part of me certainly did,
Some beautiful poems are incomplete,
some stories don't have a happy ending,
some people fall in and out of love,
some smiles fall in the way of life.

22. Everday sorrow

Head resting against the curled,
fingers of my hand,
hair on the side of my face,
pushed upward,
I think of you.

23. Longing

The touch of your dream,
upon the fine light,
someone skin was caught,
in someone else's imagined life,
nails of imagination,
scratching the back of,
somone who was never there,
but was heavy hearted,
and won't look up.
perhaps that is the only merely longing.

24. If only you could

I saw you there and I did stare,
I moved closed to you and talk a little I dare
you smiled like a flower on my first joke,
Do you remember our first our first walk?
You never stared me at my eye,
I could never understand what made you so shy?
those few talks along the pave,
the only sweet memories you gave,
wish I could live those days again,
with you beside me just for one time.

25. In between you and me

In between me you and me,
I chose you,
Between your choices and my choices,
I chose your choices,
Between the fake and the reality,
I chose the reality,
Between like and dislike,
I chose to only see myself in you,
And that was called true love,
because everything stayed between you and me,
and that's where my life ended,
and I was ready to end it happily.

26. From the heart

The night has many eyes,
and the day but one,
yet the light of bright world dies,
with the dying sun,
my mind has nearly hundred eyes,
and the heart but one,
yet the light of the whole world dies,
when the love is done.

27. You call me stranger

Its not about your body but your mere presence,
not the touch but its what I feel,
not about what you say but your voice,
Its not your lips but your warm smile is what matters,
not in my world but in reality you rule me,
not just a "friend" but a "stranger" is what pisses me,
not about the looks but it is your heart,
which has become the ruler of a part of my heart,
not every place I see you,
but you the one I see when my eyes are closed,
you are not mine because I already am yours.

28. Unsaid

I sometimes don't know what to say,
whenever I see you with someone else,
Holding hands as if noone is watching,
I wonder at times,
Do you do this just to make me feel miserable?
Is this reality which I could never see,
or is it like this is something I never wanted to see,
I smile- I laugh infront of you,
because I never want you to know that your presence around me
still bothers me,
With a smile I lead,
So that you never feel weak.

29. Deepest sea

Unhappy and empty,
Runs deeper than the deepest sea,
I got no smiles or happy times to see,
You not being in my life,
I feel empty,
But the sound of your voice,
the touch of your hand,
makes all of this go away,
as you make me smile,
you give me my heartbeat back again,
No longer I feel unhappy and empty,
deeper than the deepest sea.

30. Voice

Days pass by somehow but nights are in pain,
injuries can easily heal with upcoming time but I can assure you
the marks with remain,
restless on my bed I turn each night,
but the thoughts are hitting my head and have informed a huge
heap,
the past is flashing tearing me apart,
the darkness of my life is most visible in the dark,
and now I am trying to give it a voice,
by just trying to speak my heart.

31. Thoughts

- *Love and affection is the first pathway towards togetherness.*
- *True happiness is never gained from a wealthy pleasure but from a unique togetherness.*
- *For being happy never dwell your heart.*
- *Get busy living not busy dying.*
- *Turn. your wounds into wisdom.*
- *The criticisms make you strong.*
- *The healthies response to life is joy.*